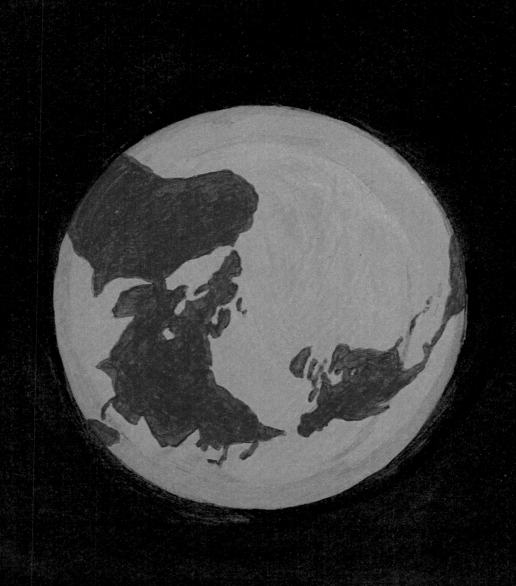

GOODBYE EARTH

A Children's Book for Grownups Who Persist

by Nancy Caye Jones

Pictures by Andy Rubin

GOODBYE EARTH A Children's Book for Grownups Who Persist
All rights reserved by Common Earth Press
Copyright July 2017

Published by Common Earth Press and Bubbie Publishing
ISBN-13: 9781548217686
ISBN-10: 1548217689

Contact information
Author: www.commonearthpress.com
Illustrator: www.andyrubin.com
Publisher: Faye@bubbiepublishing.com

Printed in the United States

for
Micah Stevie
and
Levi Emil
and
the world they will live in

In the big white house

there lives a louse

who's hugely wishing he could be

at his rich man's golf club by the sea.

In the middle of the night

he senses something isn't right.

What is wrong is in his head.

It drives him to get out of bed.

And in his bedroom all alone

he reaches for his mobile phone

to tell his followers on Twitter

that he is feeling sad and bitter.

What could it be tonight, I wonder,

that leads him to his latest blunder?

His daughter's business going bad

because she's working for her dad?

A Russian link to the election

pointing right in his direction?

A judge who's ruled against some ban?

Or those who fight his master plan

to deconstruct the world we live in

knowing that he'll be forgiven

by those who'll back him come what may

in spite of what he'll do or say?

      Go after Muslims or the press?

      Or Obama's "eight-year mess?"

Make fun of someone who's disabled?

Pick on women? Get Latinos labeled

rapists, thieves or something worse?

Build that wall from Mexico's purse?

Let's hope it's not what some folks say.

That scientists should go away.

That climate change just isn't real.

That it's a lie to spoil the deal

of Exxon and other companies

to own the earth, the soil, the seas;

to grab with greed and fill their pockets;

to frack, exploit and build their rockets.

Let's take a breath while we still can

and stand up strong against this man

who loves to bully in the night,

who cannot bear the smallest slight.

While there's still time don't let him plunder

all our land and rip asunder

treaties to protect the air

that say all nations need to share

the efforts to reverse the trend

that leads us to the very end.

        Don't let him kill the EPA.

        Don't let life just fade away.

We don't want to say goodbye

to the waters, land and sky.

We don't want to mourn and weep

and say before we go to sleep…

Goodbye panda.

Goodbye sloth.

Goodbye June bug.

Goodbye moth.

Goodbye bees.

Goodbye trees.

Goodbye jungle.

Goodbye fleas.

Goodbye coral.

Goodbye hare.

Goodbye flowers everywhere.

Goodbye turtle in the sea…

Goodbye humans, you and me.

Let it not be

The End

If you don't want to say "Goodbye Earth," please donate
to the environmental protection organization of your choice.
We do.
Nancy Caye Jones and Andy Rubin

Made in the USA
San Bernardino, CA
15 March 2019